Celebrations

Bill Batcher

To Brigidda

Bill Batcher

The Author

Bill considers himself a poet under construction. A retired teacher, with a Doctorate in Education from Teachers College, Columbia University, NY, he leads a writers group in Riverhead, NY. His poetry has been published in magazines, anthologies and online collections, and has won several awards. A book of Easter poems, *Footsteps to the Resurrection*, was published in 2005. bbatcher@optonline.net

Acknowledgements

The photograph that served as the inspiration for "Kindergarteners at the Beach" appeared on the front page of the *News-Review* [Riverhead, NY] June 17, 2010, and is used by permission of the photographer, Barbaraellen Koch.

"Spring Resurrection" appeared in *Footsteps to the Resurrection* (2005) and also in *Penned from the Heart* (2009).

"Leonids" won third place in the Autumn Poem contest, *ByLine* (2007).

"Winter" appeared in *Long Island Sounds* (2009).

"We do not know," "Annunciation," and "Like His Brothers" appeared in in *Penned from the Heart* (2007).

"Nature is Not Still" appeared in in *Penned from the Heart* (2010).

"Surveying the Garage on Ash Wednesday" appeared in *Long Island Sounds* (2010).

"Orpah" appeared in *Time of Singing* (Spring 2009).

"The Pearl Merchant" appeared in *Time of Singing* (Spring 2007) and also in *Penned from the Heart* (2010).

"Albion Rondeau" appeared in *Town Line* [South China, ME] October 4, 2003.

"Agritainment" appeared in *Paumanok: Poems and Pictures of Long Island* (2009).

"In the Waiting Room" appeared on *The Ghazal Page* (August 2006) and in *Time of Singing* (Summer 2007). It was also chosen by The Learning Federation in Australia for use in curriculum available to all schools and education systems in Australia and New Zealand.

"Writer's Villanelle" won honorable mention in the 73rd Annual *Writers Digest* Writing Competition (2004). It also appeared in *Devotions for Writers* (2008).

"Grains" appeared in *Penned from the Heart* (2009).

"Books" appeared in *Long Island Sounds* (2008).

"Triolet" won honorable mention in the 74th Annual *Writers Digest* Writing Competition (2005) and was a finalist in Long Island's Walt Whitman Contest (2007). It also appeared in *Time of Singing* (Summer 2007) and in *Devotions for Writers* (2008).

"Morning Remonstrance" appeared in *Long Island Sounds* (2009).

Bill wishes to thank the many who have encouraged him, including the ever mentoring Shirley Stevens, the faithfully critiquing Scribblers, and his understanding wife Carol.

Table of Contents

Celebrate the Season

In the summer pen a sonnet

In the summer pen a sonnet.
Write an ode to autumn's glory.
Weave a wicked winter ballad
Laying death in allegory.
Waken spring with madrigals
When the winds blow rhythm home.
Poet, put the pulse of seasons
In your mental metronome.

Cross-quarter Sevenling

We cavort around maypoles,
play hell night tricks,
and annoy sleepy groundhogs,

All because we're restless.
A season's only half over
and we wish it gone.

Relax, solstice and equinox won't be late.

April

It doesn't break a sweat or make you wear
too many woolen overcoats and hats,
(perhaps galoshes for a day, but that's
the end of it). It doesn't seem to care

it is not first or last. With thirty days
it is an average month, and none of those
are for parading flags. April agrees
to bring us Easter Morn but does not raise

a fuss if March usurps that Holy day.
Its nights are not too short and not too long
(though even equinox does not belong
on its grid). There isn't much to say,

yet in its quiet way with softened voice,
I find the days of April middling nice.

Larva Love

Each day two Eastern Tiger Swallowtails
(that's what the guidebook calls them) graze the plumes
of the butterfly bush outside our kitchen. (I assume
they are a pair). I picture once the male

a green contented caterpillar eating
his vernal days away, until by fate,
she happened on his silken trail and ate
the nearby leaf and looked toward him entreating

with her false eyes. Then he, enraptured, lifted
his fourteenth foot and pointed to my bush
so far away, and made a promise rash:
"When you and I with gossamer wings are gifted

we'll fly the million footfalls there together
and drink its precious nectar wine forever.

Spring Resurrection

Resurrection, there's no doubt,
Had to take place in Spring,
When the whole earth could celebrate,
When birds and winds could sing
And flowers prove that life returns
When seeds are tombed in earth,
And bears and wolves and porcupines
And elephants give birth,
When all of nature joins the psalm
Begun by ancient men,
That death has died, that through the Son
We can live again.

Sexting

The sun retires to her north bedroom
but leaves her warmth behind
for crickets chirping
and us strolling.
For a moment,
I see the first firefly of summer
flashing his message.

Flotsum on Sand Beach

what lobster trap
now untethered
on sea bottom
anchored this scrap
of rope

what fine wine
was caressed
by this concave
green shard
of glass

what gull
breakfasted
on this
urchin
carcass

what children
skipped laughing
dodged waves
and missed
this sand dollar

Summer

When sun insists it linger long between
horizon and horizon,
Summer says, "Let's run. Dive.
Feel warm breeze on naked legs
adorned with drops of pool-water or sweat."

But summer overstays. By mid-August,
tired of heat and clammy clothes,
I yearn for equinox
to take summer's wild ways
and let calm cool fall return.

I'm glad to see each season come
like a visiting grandchild,
and relieved to see it leave.

The Party

They worked all summer.
Pin oak, elm and maple
kept homes for birds and squirrels.
Plum, chestnut and apple
grew food for deer and man.
Their work completed,
before their winter's rest,
they celebrate the end of year
in flamboyant party dress.

Two Hunters

In cammy pants, at dusk, he sits
on his laddertop seat
among the branches;
three trees away, a red-tailed hawk
is perched.
One waits for venison. The other, mice.

Leonids

tracing fleeting filaments
we sit in adirondack chairs
double pairs of pants and blankets
guard against the morning cold

we have box seats at this show
the Leonids
burning a celestial spiderweb
one, three, nine, dozens, hundreds

at first we say 'There'
but it's no use
for when the word crosses our lips
it is not there

so we sit in silent awe
until the dawn
the others, sleeping still,
will be jealous when they hear

Powerless

What can we do without electricity?

Read,
talk,
notice wild turkeys crossing the lawn,
eat,
play,
take a brisk refreshing cold shower,
kiss,
hug,
snuggle under covers longer than usual,
think,
listen,
plan what to do when the lights come on,
watch,
laugh,
smell the fall leaves showering the lawn,
walk,
pray,
check to see if neighbors need anything,
write,
reflect,
share survival stories and count blessings.

No, we don't have electricity yet,
but we are not powerless.

Missing Guest

"Don't bring anything," our daughter said,
"I'll make it all."–Thanksgiving turkey, yams,
corn pudding, three bean salad, gravy, cran-
berry sauce, hot buttered rolls, and bread-

crumb stuffing, apple pie and pumpkin too,
with ice cream topping. What a feast she had
for all of us. But grandson Kurt looked sad.
His mother asked him, "Now what's wrong with you?"

"Where," he asked, "is Nana's spinach ring?"
–The leafy greens cooked and drained and chopped,
the eggs, swiss cheese and seasonings, served hot,
that shining green wreath Grandma *always* brings.

"I told her not to bother," our daughter said.
"You've got to be kidding!" Kurt just shook his head.

Winter

Birdsong is quiet.
Winter silences nature.
Now poets must sing.

We do not know

We do not know when Christmas was.
The Scripture doesn't say.
It could have been December, yes,
Or August, June, or May.

In winter, Christmas carries a kerosene lantern
to light the path, blazing a new trail
through virgin snow, and wears a woolen coat
and snuggles us inside.

In spring, Christmas is born again
in the scarlet tanager's nest
and peeping purple crocuses,
while warming breeze revives us.

In summer, Christmas wades in soothing ponds
and basks in warm renewing sun,
then grabs us by the hand
and bounds barefoot across a meadow.

In autumn, Christmas spreads the table
with succotash, butternut squash,
and cranberry sauce
and nourishes our hungry souls.

Annunciation

And behold, you will conceive in your womb and bear a son,
and you shall call his name Jesus. (Luke 1:31)

Take him in your inmost being,
in your womb,
carry him lovingly,
be filled with him,
be warmed as he grows within you,
and giving life,
be given life.
Become increasingly consumed
until you cannot keep him
hidden any longer.
Know you are chosen
to harbor the holy
and deliver him
to a waiting world.

Rachel's Child

An angel of the Lord appeared to Joseph in a dream and said, "Get up, take the child and his mother, and flee to Egypt,... for Herod is about to search for the child, to destroy him." (Matthew 2:13)

Another baby boy was born
in Bethlehem that Christmas morn.
His birth, no angel choir told.
No royal wise men brought him gold
or myrrh or frankincense to hold.

The searching shepherds would have found
no manger here; but all around
the little one, a family stood
and marveled how the Lord God should
have blessed them with a gift so good.

His father dreamed of years to come,–
his boy would grow up strong and some
day himself a father be.
But in these dreams he didn't see
an angel warning him to flee.

Like His Brothers

like his brethren in every respect. (Hebrews 2:17)

He ran the streets of Nazareth,
played and fell, skinned his knees,
climbed tamarisk trees,
picked ripe figs to eat
just like his brothers.

He sat and read and wondered,
asked his mother questions
about the sky, wind, and foxes,
and how he was born
just like his brothers.

He hid behind the wood pile,
worried daddy Joseph,
jumped out laughing,
ran away before he caught him
just like his brothers.

He watched men fighting over food,
women slighted at the well,
neighbors arguing about fenceposts
and strangers beaten on the road
just like his brothers.

Nature is Not Still

Lions prowl
while nervous lambs bleat

Storms brew over lakes
where fish dart and disappear

Lilies burst in sweet fragrance
and snows melt into floods

Mountains writhe
and listen to the mutterings of mustard seeds

Starlit skies whirl
in dervish dances

Nature groans
and brays
and howls
and blows
and sighs
for its sabbath rest.

January 1

aspirated short a: "Ha..."
(anticipatory pause)
[smile]
"...pinooyeer!"

After Snowfall

The snow quit falling yesterday. I see
the morning sun has baked a crust so thick
a pair of hungry cardinals who pick
for seed don't leave a trace. Not so for me

who cannot hide my footfalls as I go
to fill their feeder. Every step declares
a crunch which echoes in the oaks and scares
the very birds I've come to help. The snow

now bears a trail of holes I cannot hide:
proof that someone made the trek outside.
Soon both the sun and temperature will rise
and all those cavities will grow in size.
So if you come to check late in the day,
you'll swear a mighty giant passed this way.

Baptism

With scouring persistence, the late winter rains
kept cleansing the curbsides of weeks' blackened salt,
eroding high parkinglot mountains to plains,
providing the pigeons excuse to exalt.

Surveying the Garage on Ash Wednesday

A matching pair of bikes, "for exercise,"
resting on the wall, the rototill
for "when we plant the garden," cans filled
with years-old paint, clothes in years-old sizes,

ladders although "you're too old, You Fool,
to climb around the roof," a box of yellow-
ing paperbacks, a broken lawn umbrella,
a chaise to match, a box of rusty tools,

some furniture too beaten to allow
in the house, too good to throw away,–
"we may build a summer home some day;"–
we don't have time to sort it anyhow!

We'll get around to cleaning out our lives.
The Caravan sits outside on the drive.

Celebrate People

Kindergarteners at the Beach

fill the pail
spill the pail
watch where the water goes
mound the sand
round the sand
feel it in your toes

find a rock
find a shell
find a friend
that you can tell
learn a lesson at the beach
that wooden walls will never teach

photograph by Barbaraellen Koch, used by permission

The Captain

The Captain didn't wave when I
first drove down his street. He stared
–glared–
and watched the trespasser cruise slowly past
his number 7
number 11
number 15
and pull into the 19 drive
from which the day before his friend
moved out–
the Captain waved him on his way.

He watched me carry boxes in.
A week of moving furniture
and paintings, pots and packages
convinced the Captain I belonged
and then I too received the wave–
the wave,–and smile,–we trade each time
I pass this unpaid sentinel
who guards our one-block cul-de-sac.

Orpah

Kilion, you took me from my mother's house,
    from my father's gods.

You taught me the dances of Judah.
We ate shabas at your mother's table.
Your father sang of the hills of Zion.
You said we would go there one day.

Kilion, you took me from my mother's house,
    from my father's gods.
Now your god took you from me.

Dinner at Bethany

We catch a whiff, while walking up the street,
of Martha's barley bread, and then the lamb
and lentil stew. Inside the house is warm.
Her sister Mary helps us wash our feet,

then gives us wine; I smell the grape's bouquet.
I hear her brother talking and my breath
stops as I recall the stench of death
that filled this home last week. But we today

now celebrate new life, and from outdoors
wafts the springtime lily's sweet perfume.
All chatting stops when Christ comes in the room.
He seems more troubled than he was before;

his face looks tired, his feet worn and hard,
'til Mary breaks a fragrant pound of nard.

Grandma's Funeral

Her sisters laugh, remembering the fun
they had as kids, how she would tease and they
would get her back in kind. Her children pray,
though not for her; her struggling is done.

Not like the youngest grandkids, fully bored,
whose shirttails can't stay tucked nor bottoms seated,
until their elders' mourning is completed.
Their older siblings choose to stare at floor

than look at her, carried to the hearse.
She's not the vibrant nana who could soothe
their tears and bake their cakes and smooth
their disappointments as she ironed shirts.

Together they will miss her, gone today,
but each in his or her own private way.

Only Things

"They're only things," she said,
knee deep in the slow retreating water.
"We have our health, our lives.
They're only things," she choked.
Only things?
Family photographs,
vacations with the kids, Ausable Chasm.
The "Home is Where the Heart Is" pillow
stitched by Aunt Renee before arthritis.
Pencilled growth lines on the kitchen jamb.
Carpeting they kept the car an extra year to afford,
weeks selecting just the right color.
Books they read and hoped to read again,
but probably never would have anyway.
Hess trucks mint in box on basement shelves,
"You'll see. They'll help pay for college."
Grandma's desk earmarked for the oldest when she married.
Only things?

I Am Here

Truly I tell you, just as you did it to one of the least of these who are members of my family, you did it to me. (Matthew 25:40)

Do you see me?
in the tear-dried face of the widow
in the bloated belly of the malnourished
in the gnarled hands of the pauper

Do you hear me?
in the straining voice of the palsied
in the hacking cough of the coalminer
in the silence of the mute

Do you smell me?
in the sweated armpits of the migrant worker
in the fetid flesh of the dying
in the urine-stained clothes of the homeless

Do you feel me?
in the wizened skin of the grandmother
in the pulsing chest of the overworked
in the caked, dried feet of the traveller

Do you taste me?
in the warm stale water of the thirsty
in the dry lips of the starving
in the frustration of the hopeless

Do you sense me? I am here.

The Pearl Merchant

Again, the kingdom of heaven is like a merchant looking for fine pearls. When he found one of great value, he went away and sold everything he had and bought it. (Matthew 13:45-46)

He walked the shores of many seas;
the shellfish diggers knew his name
and waited. On the day he came
they offered their discoveries.

He scrutinized them, stone by stone,
compared and weighed, examined, sought
and analyzed,–but seldom bought,
demanding quality alone.

His knowledge of his craft was sure;
his fingers felt for any flaw;
the contour must be fully round,
the size impressive, color pure.

Yet nothing in his life before
prepared him for the pearl he found.

Transformation

Mrs. Fouad wonders when her Kareem, –
who suckled at her breast, whose smile once lit
her home, who played with every boy in town,
a kind, generous, friendly adib,–was
kidnapped by *this* Kareem she doesn't know,
who talks of jihad, war, Al-Qaeda, killing
other mothers' babies and himself.

Oblivious

He wears Air Jordans sewn by barefoot girls
outside Jakarta, twenty cents an hour,
and kicks his soccer ball across his yard,
its thirty-two panels tightly bound
with six-hundred-fifty stitches by
a boy in Sialkot, who never played.

The Spatula Man

Where do folks go when
Hunger keeps calling, and
Fickle Miss Fortune has
Left them in the lurch?
They head for the weekly
Saturday morning
Soup Kitchen Breakfast
In the basement of the church.
Here they can find a
Hot cup of coffee and
Warm friendly faces, and
Eat all they can
Of eggs and sausages,
Pancakes and home fries,
All from the grill of
The Spatula Man!
The Spatula Man!
The Spatula Man!
It's all from the grill of
The Spatula Man!

Lots of people volunteer
To help with the breakfast:
Serve cups of coffee,
Fill bowls of flakes,
Butter the bagels,
Wash down the tables,
Sweep, mop and do
Whatever it takes.
They say that it's their
Just Christian duty.
"We feel we oughta
Do what we can."
Who are they kidding?
They really come to admire
The exceptional talent of
The Spatula Man!
The Spatula Man!
The Spatula Man!
Oh, the culinary talents of
The Spatula Man!

Albion Rondeau

In Albion, one summer's day
A farmer found his fields don't pay.
Instead he built a camp/resort
For cityfolk who like to sport
Without clothes getting in the way.
These people like to work and play
Au naturel, as Frenchmen say,
On baseball field and tennis court
In Albion.

But bare behinds caused great dismay
Among the populace, so they
Asked the selectmen to exhort
All those who wish to thus cavort
To cover up or go away
From Albion.

Agritainment

Potatoes, Cauliflower,
now North Fork farmers produce a new commodity.
The bureau calls it "agritainment."

Manhattan families drive out Autumn weekends
to be agritained
with maize mazes
pumpkin picking
hay rides
scarecrow clowns.

Farmers figure, "Agritain the city folk,
sell a bushel, make a buck, send them back."
Locals don't find traffic all that agritaining.

Sunday afternoon, as audience departs
Buicks bearing bales of hay for condo lobbies
kids arguing which pumpkin
will be jack's best lantern
and Indian corn destined for office doors,
agritainers return to harvest chores.

In the Waiting Room

Arriving early, I sit by myself in the waiting room
and glance at the magazines on the shelf in the waiting room.

Highlights for Children: perennial standard–"Follow the maze
from the reindeer to the little red elf."–in the waiting room.

New Yorker: "The next day I had an appointment and would
have been in the Tower September twelfth in the waiting room."

Architectural Digest: "Seablue curtains and a renaissance frieze
coordinate with the islamic delft in the waiting room."

Men's Fitness: while I do enjoy an occasional run
I just can't visualize myself in a weight room.

Another patient arrives and sits beside me, coughing.
Here's an oxymoron for you: health in a waiting room.

When the Great Physician calls, "Bill, your turn has come,"
will I be sitting thumbing Self in the waiting room?

But Me

I

On Sunday morning
I walked into
your sanctuary
you shook my hand
handed me
a bulletin
put a welcome sticker
on my suit lapel
and showed me to a pew
beside two smiling ladies
who helped me
find the hymns.
And by the time
your maroon choir sang
the benediction
I knew I'd found
a friendly church
where all can come
and sing and pray
and all can hear
how Jesus loves sinners
and all can worship him
–but me.

II

You preached
his arms are open wide
in invitation
for all oppressed
all heavy laden.
Now I know about oppressed.
On my back
I've carried
a Dempsey Dumpster
of guilt and shame.
Whosoever may can come
–but me.

III

You sang
God so loved the world.
Now I know about love
how my throat chokes
when I find someone
who might be special
and how it churns my gut
when they walk out.
And finally finding
The One
and committing
and staying
and looking in their eyes
and knowing this is forever.
Yes,
God loves the whole world
–but me.

IV

You said Jesus ate
with publicans.
Yoo hoo!
My house is two blocks
down the road
the pink Victorian
with the wraparound porch
and I can cook
a beef wellington
you can die for.
But I know you won't come
and that's ok
for next Sunday
in your sanctuary
all will be there
to sing and pray
and worship him
–but me.

Dugout

A ten year old I visit Uncle George
in his Nebraska sod house
half in, half out of ground
rooted in the earth
like George himself

Going down into his living room
I smell earth, feel coolth
then look out a window
eyes level with grass that will become
winter wheat

Communication

Above the urinal
a message scrawled
hurriedly
indelibly
by some teen
(preteen?)
hoping
to shock or amuse
an unknown reader
with clever
single entendre.

I too scrawl
on a virtual digital wall
take time to refine
change words, images, lines
wanting, hoping
to wrest a message
to inspire or enlighten
or, yes, to shock or amuse.
But who will read it,
if anyone,
I don't, and may never, know.

Writer's Villanelle

A poet is not truly free;
I am a slave unto my pen.
A writer has to write, you see.

I can't retire, cannot flee;
I am the most enslaved of men.
A poet is not truly free.

"Ah, what a life!" Most would agree,
"I am not ruled by laws." But then
A writer has to write, you see.

I leave my desk. "It can't hold me!"
But thoughts soon pull me back again.
A poet is not truly free.

My prison is hyperbole
Or image, plot, or stratagem.
A writer has to write, you see.

In this so-called democracy
Freedom's an illusion when
A poet is not truly free.
A writer has to write, you see.

2:15 AM

What, waning gibbous moon, is your critique?
Read this poem aloud and give report.
The iambic pentameter too weak?
Too stilted? Is the poem too long? too short?

This starlit lakeside night, I cannot sleep.
You summon me from bed, oh gibbous moon.
I'd rather make a date you cannot keep
At 2:15 tomorrow afternoon.

Should I abandon sonnet? Try free verse?
The opening lunar metaphor, cliché?
Do all these questions only make it worse?
Do I have really anything to say?
Give, waning gibbous moon, your tough advice.
Do I write poems that matter, or sound nice?

The Sudoku Player

She	works	the	morning	puzzle	——in	ink,	checks	her
book	of	jigsaws,	ABCs,	overlaps,	and	killers	for	undone
pages,	and	goes	online	to	compete	with	faceless	players.
Eggs	for	breakfast	eliminates	that	candidate	for	lunch	and
supper,	and	also	fills	her	husband's	meal	cells.	Does
it	predestine	all	the	open	cells	for	the	day?
She	chooses	her	diet	with	care.	Born	in	1945,
she	is	resolved	to	live	'til	2036	(or	7
or,	8),	so	her	headstone	won't	repeat	any	digits.

Celebrate the Moment

Mountain Faith

*I tell you the truth, if you have faith as small as a mustard seed, you can say to this mountain,
'Move from here to there' and it will move. Matthew 17:20*

My faith says to mountain,
"You stay right where you are, thank you very much.
Don't go skipping across the valley on my account,
scaring all the townfolk, worrying the deer,
confusing the eagle who's been fishing all day
and expects her lofty nest to be right there
where she left it."

Un-Nature Center

The fur that used to slink through woods
pursuing dinner now drapes on countertop
while on the wall a mounted shark swims motionless.
A giant snakeskin props beside the window
in front of comfortable couches
and turtles stop swimming laps in their six foot tank
to sun beneath a lamp.
The skulls and bones in tabletop display
do not decay
but whisper "Touch me. Guess what I was–once."

Shore Breeze

the breeze seems too light
to make these waves
lap the shore

like a passing tanker
whose wake continues
to stir the water
long after it has passed
from view

perhaps these waves
continue to respond
to wind now quiet

Freedom

CbAiGrEd

C AbGiErd

C A GbEird

C A G Ebird

C A G E   bird

C A G E

Beehive

We sit on rough-hewn granite blocks
on the parking lot's periphery
and stare up at the mountain.
I'm the first to notice and try
to point her eyes to the dot of red
inching its way across a rock face
from one clump of trees to another
a dot of light blue following.

I imagine red dot calling encouragement
to light blue, "not much further"
grasping the eighty-year old iron rods
feeling the breeze
and occasionally stopping to look down
at Sand Beach
and two dark blue dots
on the edge of the parking lot.

Grains

You are the salt of the earth. (Matthew 5:13)
The kingdom of heaven is like yeast. (Matthew 13:33)

Seventy sextillion stars
in ten thousand galaxies
So what am I?
Thirteen billion elbows
So what am I?
a dust speck
   ocean ripple
   flea blink
   Yosemite twig
a single pulse
a hemidemisemiquaver
a frayed thread
   forgotten thought
   whispered schwa
   penciled tittle
a grain of sand.

He says to me,
Not sand, but salt.
Not sand, but yeast.

Books

A new book has a captivating smell
Of mystery, of intrigue, and of wonder,
Luring to its secrets hidden well
The reader unaware the spell you're under.

An old book has a friendly handshake feel,
"So good to see once more the one I miss.
Let's share again our stories. Come let's seal
Our friendship with a cup of reminisce."

A lost book is like a half-forgotten song
A snatch of which you often find you're singing.
You likely have the melody all wrong.
You can't recall the ending or beginning.
Once read, a book forever haunts your brain.
A lot is lost but parts of it remain.

where are the caps?

maybe im humble and dont think
my words merit upper case
im a lc type of guy

or i think im being artsy
where do i think im cummings from

or shift key broke or my pinkys
too lazy to press it down
no look at the question mark
i needed shift for that
i must have had a reason

Artesian Well

Throughout the day, cars park beside the road.
The endless flowing water from the pipe
fills empty jars and bottles, each in turn.
Between the jars, spills extra on the rocks.
When each one takes his stolen gallon home
the fountain measures not a gallon less.

One driver stops to fill his thirsty hands
and tastes the cold refreshing stream again.
The only vessel that he brought
to bring the water home,–himself.

Throughout the night when cars are all garaged,
the water bubbles wastefully away.

Triolet

She reads, I write and all is still
for nothing breaks our quietude.
Disturb the other, neither will.
She reads, I write and all is still.
The turning page, the flowing quill:
the only sounds that dare intrude.
She reads, I write and all is still
for nothing breaks our quietude.

Seawall

The sea threw up a stony wall on shore
of beachball boulders, scoured seagull white
by centuries of sea and surf, packed tight
by constant jostling, a well-tamped olive jar.

Today we stop to sit atop the mound.
A watchful gull selects a nearby rock
and listens for the crinkle of a sack
of chips. Ignoring him, we look around.

Men build walls to keep outsiders out,
insiders in, to mark where kitchen ends
and bath begins, and every son defends
his small domain with warnings to all about.

What motive does the sea have up her sleeve?
We toss the gull a pretzel. Then we leave.

Redemption

The auctioneer gavels "Sold!"
Soon the barn, as barn, won't be.
Its broad proud planks
paneling for a living room.
Its utile beams artistic ornament.
Its land freed for
more valued real estate.

"But," one voice inquires,
"won't you sell
the privies too?"

Storm-beaten,
poison-ivy-covered,
urine splattered, splintered boards,
doors with rusted springs
and turn-block latch
built for shit,
now prizes in a bidding war.

Morning Remonstrance

Yesterday's dishes I won't put away
    though they're thoroughly dry in the rack
For I know they'll demolish the mood of the day
    if I should start putting them back.

No matter how gently I place them in piles
    the plates will not quietly go;
They are being imprisoned without a fair trial
    and they want the whole household to know.

The cups and the saucers demanding their rights
    in protest will shout loud and clear.
"Though melmac and styrofoam keep out of sight,
    we're china, we're proud and we're here."

The glasses, for their part, are sneaky today;
    these girlish sopranos conspire,
If I take two or three to the cabinet, then they
    will become a boisterous bell choir.

I take hold of a knife or a fork or a spoon
    and regardless how much I implore,
It insists on clanging objection as soon
    as I lower it into the drawer.

The casserole covers, when put on the shelves,
    continue complaining. I'm sure
That the pots and the pans consider themselves
    percussion for some overture.

If I can preserve for this little while
    some peace, then I'm going to try.
So instead of getting the dishes all riled,
    I elect to let sleeping bowls lie.

Made in the USA
Charleston, SC
27 October 2014